RAPTORS
THE EAGLES, HAWKS, FALCONS, AND OWLS OF NORTH AMERICA

A COLORING ALBUM

ANNE PRICE

RAPTOR ILLUSTRATIONS BY **DONALD MALICK**

AND ADDITIONAL WORK BY **RANDY SIMONS**

FOREWORD BY **ROGER TORY PETERSON**

ROBERTS RINEHART PUBLISHERS,

IN COOPERATION WITH THE **RAPTOR EDUCATION FOUNDATION**

DEDICATION

For Alexander, Connor, Glenna, and all of you other kids at heart who have ever been charmed by talons and hooked beaks…

THE RAPTOR EDUCATION FOUNDATION IN THE 21ST CENTURY

"The only wildlife theater company in America promoting science"

The Raptor Education Foundation (REF) ™ has been promoting environmental literacy since 1980 by providing schools, corporations, conventions, and gatherings of all sizes unique programs and seminars that connect people with the natural world. REF utilizes an extensive cast of live, non-releasable raptors to focus attention on environmental concepts and issues.

In 1999, working with Colorado legislators, Colorado's Governor Owens and numerous county officials, REF designed and issued Colorado's first-ever motor vehicle license plates featuring an environmental/wildlife theme and benefiting REF's environmental literacy mission. The *Colorado Respects Wildlife* license plates are available only to qualified REF members. The beautiful graphics featuring America's national symbol, promote REF's mission on the streets and highways of Colorado as part of REF's ongoing *Driving For Wildlife* campaign.

The Foundation operates as a non-profit 501 (c) (3) educational organization with special permits issued by the U.S. Fish and Wildlife Service and the Colorado Division of Wildlife. REF has received numerous awards and commendations for its programs. In 2005, Anne Price, REF's curator of raptors received international acclaim by being featured in the world's oldest continually published sportsmen's magazine, *Ohota* in Russia. Since its inception, REF has been self-supporting, without relying on state or federal dollars.

A small staff, along with highly-trained and dedicated docents, provide programs and services across the United States and abroad. Members are found world wide. Corporate and foundation partners include Panwy Foundation, Wolf Creek Charitable Foundation, Vail Valley Foundation, Beaver Creek Resort, Virginia Wellington Cabot Foundation, Robert R. McCormick Tribune Foundation, El Pomar Foundation, ARCO, Chevron, Total Petroleum, and the California Academy of Sciences, to name a few.

To achieve its goals and continue its environmental literacy programs into its third decade, REF needs your help. You may support our efforts through membership, donations, and volunteerism.

FOR FURTHER INFORMATION:

WEB SITES:
www.usaref.org
www.drivingforwildlife.org
www.raptoreducationfoundation.org

E-MAIL:
raptor2@usaref.org

PHONE:
303-680-8500

FAX:
303-680-8502

ADDRESS:
P.O. Box 200400
Denver, Colorado 80220
USA

PUBLISHED BY:
ROBERTS RINEHART PUBLISHERS
A member of the Rowman and Littlefield Publishing Group
4501 Forbes Boulevard, Suite 200
Lanham, MD 20706

DISTRIBUTED BY:
NATIONAL BOOK NETWORK

ISBN-13: 978-1-57098-405-1
ISBN-10: 1-57098-405-0

BOOK DESIGN:
Ann W. Douden, PO Box 502, Fraser, Colorado 80442

FRONT COVER:
Barred Owl, *Strix varia*, Digital Photo by Peter Reshetniak

Contents

ACKNOWLEDGMENTS

The first version of this book sold over 66,000 copies, and I am grateful to everyone for helping the Raptor Education Foundation spread its wings and its message. Don Malick's illustrations continue to set standards for accuracy while capturing the spirit of his favorite birds, and I am pleased we can include brand new illustrations in this revised edition. Don had prepared these for the original book, but they could not be included because of size constraints. Just a few months after Don completed his illustrations, he succumbed to his battle with cancer. We have also kept the applicable parts of Roger Tory Peterson's original foreword, as he knew better than most the remarkable quality of Don's work. Since the first edition was printed, Roger Tory Peterson and Dr. Frances Hamerstrom, the original author and reknowned researcher, have passed away. My fantasy is that all of them are in a blind somewhere, enjoying the birds that were so instrumental in connecting their lives with mine and everyone else who loves raptors and the natural world.

Randy Simons' faithful copies of Don's illustrations still resonate perfectly with the originals. Randy lives on the plains of eastern Colorado where his fly fishing adventures bring him into regular contact with all kinds of wildlife, including a fishing Great Horned Owl.

Anne Price took on writing the new text under the intense demands of motherhood with three month-old Glenna and three year-old Connor; working as Curator of REF's raptor collection, and training our docents. Very special thanks are given to husband Doug for helping her do all of that and more.

Special acknowledgement is due Seven Hills Veterinary Center, Aurora, Colorado; especially Drs. Jeff Mullen, Mike Ley, and Matt Demey for the excellent health care they provide REF's raptors. Also, Dr. James C. Bednarz, the editor of *The Journal of Raptor Research*, graciously provided final confirmation for taxonomic listings.

For over twenty five years certain people and organizations have been instrumental in allowing REF to keeps its doors open, to continue paying its bills, and forging on despite the many obstacles associated with running any enterprise, especially a small non-profit. Marie Bolster leads this group with her multifaceted generosity and ability to keep me focused during stressful times with her wonderful sense of humor. Special thanks are owed David and Nancy Wyman and the Panwy Foundation for their steadfast financial support, trust, and willingness to stick with us in tough times. Pat O'Brien of Chevron Research and Technology has been a stalwart in generously supporting our message, as have Bob and Roxanne Koehler, Helen Johnson, Randy Simons, Alexander and Eugenie Reshetniak, Mary Anne Mills, Susan Raymond, Greg Septon, Sherrie York, Terry Grosz, Kent Ullberg, and William F. Greve, Jr. We are also grateful to the Bar N I Ranch, for support of our education programs, and our highly dedicated group of docents who multiply our impact a hundredfold. Thanks are also due to the good people at the U.S. Fish & Wildlife Service and the Colorado Division of Wildlife for their hard work in preserving the "thin green line" that helps our wildlife maintain some small toehold in an environment subjected to the ever-expanding appetites of civilization.

Peter Reshetniak
President
Raptor Education
Foundation

FOREWORD

The birds of prey, especially the eagles, are the aristocrats of the bird world, surveying the earth as they soar in the sky. We often speak of them as raptors, which include the eagles, osprey, hawks, falcons and also the vultures, which really are scavengers, not hunters. Owls are not related but they fill the nocturnal niche. Like the day-flying birds of prey they have hooked beaks and talons.

Hawks and eagles have eyes that are 8 or 9 times as sharp as human eyes. On the other hand owls depend on ears that are far more sensitive than ours, pinpointing their prey in the dark.

When I was a young man, about 50 years ago, we knew of only a few vantage points where we could watch hawks in migration—notably Point Pelee on Lake Erie, Cape May Point in New Jersey, and Hawk Mountain in Pennsylvania. In recent years raptor watchers, like other birdwatchers, have become legion and now congregate at more than 200 vantage points across the land where they can observe large numbers of migrating birds of prey during spring and fall. On the other hand, owl watchers, or rather owl listeners, often prowl around at night with their tape recorders.

Don Malick, the artist, lives in Colorado where for 12 years he was associated with the Denver Museum of Natural History. Inspired and influenced by the late George Sutton, he is one of the strongest draftsmen amongst those who are painting wildlife today. He knows how a bird is put together—its underlying musculature and surface pterylography (arrangement of feathers). This is very evident in these line drawings which are structurally strong and give us the characteristic look or "jizz" of each species.

No one has painted birds of prey—or woodpeckers, or many other birds for that matter—better than Don Malick. His bird portraiture is featured extensively in Bailey's *Birds of Colorado* and in the National Geographic Society's new bird guide. But aside from the raptors his great love has always been the birds of Africa. His expeditions to Botswana in southern Africa gave him free reign to paint more expansively and his field studies made in that wild region are superb.

This coloring book will make you more sensitive to the overall appearance and the patterns of these magnificent birds. You may find colored pencils easiest to use; but if you can handle brushes and watercolor you might prefer to use that medium. Crayons, too, can be used. The important thing is to enjoy the exercise. But don't be just an armchair devotee of the raptors. Go out, preferably with a binocular, sharpen your vision, and let your spirit soar.

In purchasing this book your contribution will enable the Raptor Education Foundation to expand its educational programs in North America. Keep the eagles flying!

Editors Note: Excerpted from the 1984 original.

Roger Tory Peterson.

HOW TO USE THIS BOOK

Raptors are the ideal "first bird" for a child interested in nature. They are big, slow, and relatively easy to spot. For a younger child, this activity book will aid in learning to tell the difference between an owl and an eagle, for instance. Older children can appreciate the "COOL FACTS" about each bird, which cover a wide range of topics from how the bird was named to some of the more interesting hunting techniques employed by raptors. Advanced vocabulary words are in bold the first time they are introduced and included in the glossary on page 7. Encourage your budding artist to notice the different body shapes of each bird, and then let them create their own unique species using colors of their choice. The color plates need not be the final answer, as children perceive the world far differently than we adults do. Finally, use this book as a bridge to field guides and other resources about raptors and wildlife. Keep your eyes up, and who knows? Your child may spot his or her first hawk before you do!

WHAT MAKES A BIRD A RAPTOR?

Raptors are predatory birds, meaning they kill other animals for food. But many birds are **carnivorous**, or meat-eaters. Raptors are distinguished by their incredibly strong, grasping feet, tipped with sharp **talons**. They use their feet to catch and kill their **prey**, unlike other predatory birds such as herons, which use their beaks.

All raptors are excellent fliers, either because they need to chase down prey, sneak up on it, or soar long distances looking for it. Some raptors, like the **accipiters**, are good at flying very fast for short distances. Owls have very soft feathers which muffle sound, and their flight is silent. Vultures and some eagles have long, broad wings that allow them to soar for hundreds of miles.

CERE

MALAR STRIPE

BREAST

BELLY

COVERT FEATHERS

TALONS

PRIMARIES

TAIL

GLOSSARY

Accipiter: the genus name of forest hawks with short, round wings and long tails

Buteo: the genus name of soaring hawks with long, broad wings and short tails

Carnivorous: eating meat

Carrion: meat from the body of a dead animal

Class: a group of animals below a phylum and above an order, with common physiologies. All birds are in the class Aves, all mammals in the class Mammalia, all reptiles in the class Reptilia, and so on.

Clutch: the total number of eggs that a bird lays at one time

Crepuscular: active at sunrise and sunset

Diurnal: active during daylight hours

Endangered: animals so few in number that they may not reproduce enough to survive

Extinct: a species which no longer survives anywhere on earth, such as dinosaurs

Eyass: a baby raptor from the time it hatches until it can crawl or hop out of the nest

Eyrie: a raptor nest, usually one on the edge of a cliff

Facial Disk: the special feathers surrounding an owl's eyes and beak, curved to form half-circles on each side. They absorb and direct sound towards the owl's ears.

Family: groups of animals within an order. Bird families are grouped according to shapes of the beak, lengths of feathers, structure of the feet, and genetic similarity.

Falconry/Falconer: a person who hunts wild game using a trained raptor

Fossil: the remains of an animal or plant from a past geologic age, preserved in the ground

Genus: groups of animals within a family. Bird genera (plural) show close relationships within a family, including anatomical features and behavioral traits.

Habitat: the type of environment where an animal normally lives, including climate and vegetation

Immature: describing a bird that is not yet ready to breed, but is no longer dependent on its parents

Kingdom: the broadest, most general category for grouping organisms. All animals are in the kingdom Animalia.

Malar stripe: a dark patch or line of feathers under the eye of (usually) a falcon, for reducing the glare of the sun

Migrate: to travel to another region or habitat in search of a better climate and food, usually when the season changes

Mimic: to imitate another creature in appearance, sound or action

Morph: the particular permanent coloring of a raptor which varies from most members of that species, i.e., in buteos, there are "light morph" and "dark morph" birds

Nocturnal: active during the night

Order: a group of animals below a class and above a family, which resemble each other structurally. Similar features include the shape of the bones in the skull and the chest.

Ornithologist: a person who studies birds

Parasite: tiny animals that live off the bodies (either inside or outside) of other animals

Phylum: a group of animals below a kingdom and above a class. All animals with a spinal cord are in the phylum Chordata.

Prey: the animal food that a raptor catches and eats

Raptor: a meat-eating bird that has a hooked beak and strong, grasping feet with talons

Species: a population of animals which can breed and produce offspring that also can breed. Normally, species do not interbreed in the wild.

Spicules: special rough skin scales on the underside of an Osprey's foot for holding on to fish

Stoop: a high-speed, steep dive made by a raptor, usually while chasing prey

Subspecies: a geographic variation of a species. Subspecies can interbreed, but normally do not do so because they have evolved in isolation of one another. For instance, the Barn Owls found in Europe are a different subspecies than those in the United States, and do not interbreed because the Atlantic Ocean separates them.

Tail-chase: when a raptor chases another bird directly from behind, following its every move

Talons: the sharp claws at the end of a raptor's toes

Wingspan: the total width of a bird's wings, from the tip of the left wing, across the back, to the tip of the right wing

BIRD OR DINOSAUR?

Raptors and all other birds are believed to be descended from some kind of small dinosaur that ran on two legs and lived about 220 million years ago during the Triassic Period. But which dinosaur? Are modern birds really living dinosaurs, or simply animals that evolved from reptiles? Scientists are still trying to figure out all of these questions, and the **fossil** record is very incomplete. There are many things that reptiles and birds have in common, including scales, similar bones in the skull and ribs, and even their red blood cells. But there are differences too. Birds are warm-blooded and have a heart with four separate chambers, and reptiles are cold-blooded with a three-chambered heart. Only birds have feathers, and some scientists think that feathers may have evolved to help keep birds warm.

The earliest known fossil of a bird is *Archaeopteryx lithographica*, discovered in Europe in 1861. This creature was part bird and part reptile, and probably would have been considered a small dinosaur except for the fact that it had feathers. The bones in its hips, legs and shoulders were pretty similar to modern birds, but it had a long bony tail, teeth and clawed fingers, like a reptile. Scientists aren't even sure if *Archaeopteryx* could fly. Some think that maybe it just glided down out of trees, like modern flying squirrels do.

Raptors first appeared in the fossil record at the very beginning of the Tertiary Period, about 65 million years ago. Owls seemed to have evolved before hawks, eagles and kites, and falcons didn't appear until much later. Like the dinosaurs, there are several species of raptors which have gone **extinct**, including Haast's Eagle, the largest eagle that ever lived. This bird lived in New Zealand, and weighed about 30 pounds. It preyed on large, flightless birds called "moas", which were up to ten feet tall. Both the eagle and the moas went extinct when people first came to the islands, about 1000 years ago. Men killed the moas for food, and since moas couldn't fly, they were easy prey. But scientists think they may have also killed the eagles to protect themselves, since the eagles killed moas that were as big as, and even bigger than humans!

1

2

3

4

The eggs on page 9 come from an owl, a falcon, an eagle, and a hawk. Look at the sizes and see if you can match the eggs, to the feet, to the feathers. For further clues go to our web site at www.usaref.org and research the site for the answers. The first 50 correct answers (matching the numbers/letters with proper picture) mailed to REF offices will receive a beautiful eagle pin.

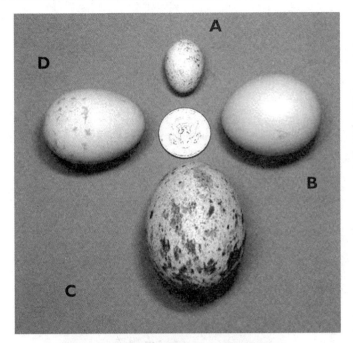

WHAT ABOUT THESE FUNNY NAMES?

You'll notice that beneath each of the species' names in this book, there is another, two-word name in italic letters. This is the "scientific" name of the bird, which comes from the Greek and Latin languages. This system of naming and classifying organisms was developed by Carolus Linnaeus, a Swedish naturalist who lived in the 18th century. Using the scientific names works much better, because common names vary from one place to another. For instance, the Black Vulture of India and the Black Vulture of the United States are two completely different birds, but if you say "*Coragyps atratus,*" everyone knows exactly which bird you're talking about, even if you're speaking two different languages! The scientific names are made up of two parts, and sometimes a third. The first name is the **genus**, which is always capitalized, and the second name is the **species**. The third name, if used, is the **subspecies** of the organism.

All organisms are classified, or arranged in a very specific way, from the broadest category to the most specific. Here's how it works with the Bald Eagle:

Kingdom:	Animalia	(all animals)
Phylum:	Chordata	(animals with a bundle of nerves running down the top surface of the back)
Class:	Aves	(all birds)
Order:	Falconiformes	(all diurnal raptors)
Family:	Accipitridae	(eagles, hawks, kites, Old World vultures)
Genus:	Haliaeetus	(sea eagles)
Species:	leucocephalus	(means "white headed")

So, the scientific name of the Bald Eagle is *Haliaeetus leucocephalus,* which comes from the Greek words meaning, "white-headed sea eagle". The subspecies found in Alaska and Canada is *Haliaeetus leucocephalus alascensis.*

Summer Distribution Map Examples

Mississippi Kite:*Ictinia mississippiensis*

Prairie Falcon: *Falco mexicanus*

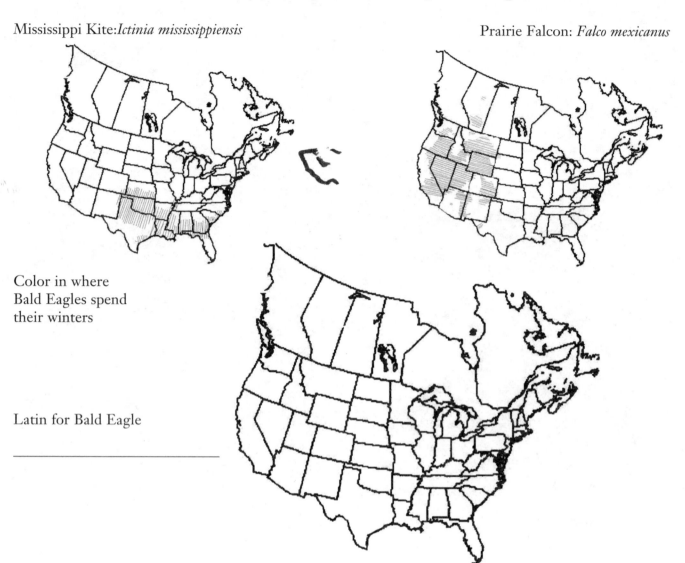

Color in where
Bald Eagles spend
their winters

Latin for Bald Eagle

_____

Broad-winged Hawk: *Buteo platypterus*

Harris' Hawk: *Parabuteo unicinctus*

*For distribution maps of North America's raptors go to the Patuxent Wildlife
Research Center (PWRC) web site: www.mbr-pwrc.usgs.gov/. Remember,
distribution maps change according to the seasons as raptors migrate to find prey.*

EAGLES

Bald Eagle
Haliaeetus leucocephalus

The Bald Eagle is the living national symbol of the United States of America, chosen by the founding fathers in 1782. It isn't really "bald", of course. It has a full head of snowy white feathers once it becomes an adult, at about 4 to 5 years of age. For many years, Bald Eagles were an **endangered** species. By educating people about Bald Eagles and protecting eagle **habitat**, scientists and other concerned citizens helped the Bald Eagle recover. There are now about 50,000 adult eagles in the United States.

COOL FACT:

An adult female Bald Eagle can have a wingspan of up to 8 feet. That's bigger than the tallest basketball player!

PLM

Golden Eagle

Aquila chrysaetos

The Golden Eagle gets its name from the beautiful light golden feathers on the top of the head and back of the neck. They live all around the world in the Northern Hemisphere, or the upper half of the globe, in wide open spaces like plains, deserts and mountain slopes. Goldens are large, powerful eagles that hunt small and medium-sized mammals like ground squirrels and jackrabbits, but they can even kill a small deer or antelope if they are very hungry and try hard enough.

COOL FACT:

Even though Golden Eagles lay two eggs, usually only one chick, or **eyass** survives. The older eyass that hatches first almost always kills the second one. This is called the "Cain-Abel Syndrome."

OSPREY

Osprey
Pandion haliaetus

The Osprey is one of the most unusual raptors in the world. Neither a typical hawk, nor a true eagle, it is in a special family all by itself. Ospreys eat only fish, and unlike most sea eagles, they will actually dive, feet first, all the way under the water to catch their prey. They are found worldwide, and soar with their wings "crooked", or slightly bent at the wrist. That's one of the easy ways to tell them apart from Bald Eagles, which soar on flat, straight wings.

COOL FACT:

Ospreys can swivel the outer toes on each foot. They also have special, rough scales on the bottom of their feet called **spicules.** Both adaptations mean Ospreys are very good at holding on to slippery fish!

VULTURES

California Condor

Gymnogyps californianus

Condors are very large vultures, and the California Condor is the largest raptor in the United States. They have been soaring on warm winds looking for **carrion**, since the last Ice Age. Females can have wingspans of nearly 10 feet, and weigh up to 31 pounds. The California Condor is also the most endangered raptor in the United States. In 1987 the few remaining wild Condors were captured and taken to breeding centers. Scientists, trying to increase the population, carefully bred these birds, but since Condors lay only one egg every two years, it took some time before people felt there were enough Condors to risk releasing some back to the wild. Eight were released in southern California in 1992, and in 1996, 6 birds were released at Vermillion Cliffs in Arizona. Hopefully these birds will survive and reproduce, and the California Condor will not become extinct.

COOL FACT:

Condors will sometimes fly hundreds of miles each day in search of food. In 1998, an **immature** Condor wandered all the way from Utah to western Colorado! Bird watchers and **ornithologists** were very excited, and many came from far away, just to catch a glimpse of a live, wild Condor.

NEWS FLASH!

Scientists studying the genetic molecules called "DNA" of New World vultures like the California Condor and Turkey Vulture discovered that the closest relatives of these vultures are actually storks, not other raptors!

Turkey Vulture
Cathartes aura

Turkey vultures are large, graceful birds with bare heads. Although their wingspans are nearly as big as an eagle's, they weigh only half as much, about four pounds. Because vultures eat carrion, they have special adaptations which allow them to stay clean and healthy. Bare heads mean that old, sticky meat won't cling to eyes, ears or the nose. And speaking of vulture noses, you can see right through the nose of a Turkey Vulture! The hole in the cartilage is large enough to shake out a piece of meat. Standing on a rotten carcass for several hours might cause an infection on their feet, so even Turkey Vulture "doo-doo" has a special function: it kills bacteria, and runs right down the vulture's legs!

COOL FACT:

Turkey Vultures are one of the few raptors in the world that can **smell.** They use their sharp sense of smell, as well as their eyes, to locate food.

Black Vulture

Coragyps atratus

   The Black Vulture is slightly smaller than the Turkey Vulture, but if there is a large, dead animal to be feasted on, the Black Vulture is boss. Black Vultures will sleep together at night, and chase Turkey Vultures away from a kill. They will also kill live prey with their beaks, such as fish and even newborn pigs. Although they can't smell, they have keen vision which helps them locate their food, which they sometimes do by watching the actions of other scavengers like ravens, magpies and coyotes.

COOL FACT:

Black Vultures will occasionally eat palm fruit,
and other vegetable matter they find rotting in dumps.

KITES

Snail Kite
Rostrhamus sociabilis

   The Snail Kite gets its name because it eats almost nothing but apple snails. They have very thin, sharply hooked upper beaks which they use to pry the snails out of their shells. Snail Kites are found in the Everglades region of Florida, but they are also found in marshlands of Mexico, Cuba and Central and South America. If there is a drought in Florida, Snail Kites will range all through the state looking for wet marshes and food.

COOL FACT:

When a Snail Kite spots a snail on the water's surface, it swoops down, and grabs the snail with its talons. Still flapping, it then transfers the snail from its foot to its beak, never stopping to land!

Swallow-Tailed Kite
Elanoides forficatus

The Swallow-Tailed Kite is found in the extreme southeastern United States along the Gulf coast. They build nests and raise babies from about April until September, and then they **migrate** south to Venezuela and Argentina for the winter. They get their name from their long, deeply-forked tails. Swallow-Tailed Kites are spectacular flyers, catching prey like insects on the wing, then transferring the food to their beaks to eat. As a matter of fact, they spend so much time flying that their feet are quite small, and they sometimes have trouble standing! But they are very good at maneuvering in forests and swamps, and can snatch lizards and snakes right off of branches.

COOL FACT:

When a boy wants to impress a girl, he may bring her flowers. But when a male Swallow-Tailed Kite wants to impress a female, he brings her an "anole," a small green lizard!

Mississippi Kite
Ictinia mississippiensis

The Mississippi Kite is also found in the southeastern United States, but it will wander north to the eastern Great Plains states, and even as far west as Arizona during the summer months. Like most kites, it catches a variety of prey, and is very good at snagging grasshoppers, cicadas and even dragonflies right out of the air. They are very social birds, and will sleep and hunt together in small flocks. Mississippi Kites will also hunt turtles, small birds and bats.

COOL FACT:

In places like Texas, Oklahoma and Kansas, the Mississippi Kite has learned to follow and hang around herds of antelope, cattle and bison. The herds kick up insects from the grass, which the kites then swoop down and capture.

White-Tailed Kite

Elanus leucurus

From a distance, the White-Tailed Kite can sometimes be confused for a gull. Gray and white, with an erratic, disorganized flight, most White-Tailed Kites are found along the California and Texas coasts, along with many species of gulls! The old name for this bird was the Black-Shouldered Kite, for the black upperwing feathers which look like "shoulders" when the kite is perched. This beautiful little raptor hunts rodents almost exclusively, unlike many other kites which also feed on insects and reptiles.

COOL FACT:

While hunting, White-Tailed Kites will turn into the wind and hover for several seconds, looking for rodents below. When something is spotted, the kite lowers it feet, and raises its wings over its head in a deep "V", and drops like a rock into the tall grass.

FALCONS

Gyrfalcons are probably the fastest animals in the world. People who have trained them for **falconry** estimate that they can dive or **stoop** out of the sky chasing prey at around 200 miles per hour!

Gyrfalcon
Falco rusticolus

The Gyrfalcon is the largest falcon in the world. They live in the Arctic, and are very well adapted to survive in the harsh, cold climate. Gyrfalcons will migrate south to the northern United States and Europe during the winter, looking for food like grouse, ptarmigan and ducks. There are three color **morphs** found in the wild: gray birds are found in Canada, black ones in the Labrador region, and the snow-white birds in Iceland and Greenland.

Peregrine Falcon
Falco peregrinus

About 4000 years ago, people learned to train falcons, hawks and eagles to hunt animals for them. This very ancient sport is called falconry. **Falconers** all over the world have flown peregrines for centuries, and the practice continues today. Peregrines hunt by stooping out of the sky at very high speeds, and smashing into their prey with their long yellow toes curled up like a fist. In the 1950s, man began using a poison called DDT to kill insects. The DDT washed off the land and into the water, and eventually got into the bodies of many meat-eating birds like the Peregrine Falcon. Some falcons died, but the DDT also made the falcon eggs so thin that they cracked when the parents sat on them to keep them warm. Their numbers dwindled, and they became an endangered species. By stopping the use of DDT and breeding many baby falcons for release in the wild, people have saved the Peregrine from extinction.

COOL FACT:

The word "peregrine" is from a Latin word that means "wanderer, stranger or foreigner". Peregrines migrate long distances, and are found on every continent except Antarctica!

Prairie Falcon
Falco mexicanus

The Prairie Falcon is a beautiful sandy brown and cream-colored falcon. It lays its eggs in shallow scrapes called **eyries** or **aeries** on the edges of cliffs and bluffs. Like most falcons, Prairie Falcons have **malar** stripes, or dark markings under their eyes. These work just like sunglasses, cutting down on the glare from the sun. And there is plenty of sun in the vast, lonely places of the American West where Prairie Falcons live.

COOL FACT:
Most falcons hunt other birds, as does the Prairie Falcon. But they also eat ground squirrels, which they catch by flying very low to the ground, using the land for cover.

Aplomado Falcon
Falco femoralis

The Aplomado Falcon used to nest in the American southwest, but due to the destruction of its habitat, it is now only occasionally seen in southwest Texas and Arizona. This falcon will do whatever it takes to catch its meal, which is usually small birds. It will stoop like other large falcons, **tail-chase** like Kestrels and Merlins, and even crash through heavy brush, chasing prey on foot! Aplomado Falcons have also learned to hunt for insects, rodents and reptiles at the edge of grassfires, waiting for the fleeing animals.

COOL FACT:

The word "Aplomado" means "lead-colored" in Spanish, referring to the color on the back and wings of this falcon.

Merlin
Falco columbarius

The Merlin is the second smallest falcon found in the U.S. Unlike most other falcons, they have very pale malar marks on their faces. They feed almost exclusively on birds, which they catch by tail-chasing at high speeds. Male Merlins have grayish backs, heads and wings, but the females are brown.

COOL FACT:

Merlins were popular for falconry in the Middle Ages and Renaissance. They were known as a lady's falcon, and nuns even brought their Merlins to church with them!

American Kestrel
Falco sparverius

American Kestrels are the smallest falcons found in the U.S. An adult male weighs about four ounces! This tiny falcon used to be called a "sparrowhawk", but they are true falcons, with pointed wings, a long tail, and double malar stripes on each side of their faces. They catch many types of small prey, such as finches, sparrows, mice, lizards and grasshoppers. Because they eat many different animals and can adapt well to man's presence, American Kestrels are the most common raptor in the U.S. They even nest in cities.

COOL FACT:

Kestrels are one of the few raptors in the world that can hover. Many times you can see them fluttering over a field, but staying in one place in the sky. They're looking for something to eat!

Crested Caracara
Caracara plancus

The Crested Caracara is the national bird of Mexico. Although it is a member of the falcon family, it behaves and looks much more like a vulture than a falcon. It has large, broad wings for soaring, a bare face, a thick beak and long legs. They hunt small birds, mammals, reptiles, amphibians and insects, and also scavenge for carrion. Caracaras live on the prairies of south Texas and central Florida, and are also occasionally found in Arizona and New Mexico.

COOL FACT:

Caracaras will often "pirate" or steal food from other raptors. They will even harass vultures, forcing them to regurgitate their food so they can steal an easy meal!

HARRIERS

Northern Harrier
Circus cyaneus

The old name for this raptor is "Marsh Hawk", which suited the bird well, since they hunt and nest in wet, open areas. Harriers are another raptor which can hover, and there is a military jet named for them which can take off and land vertically, as well as hover. The males mostly hunt small birds, and are gray, with black-tipped wings. The females take more mammals, and are brown with dark streaks on their bellies and breasts. The word "harrier" comes from an Old English term that means to harass by hostile attacks, which describes how these birds hunt. They fly very low over the grass, moving back and forth, repeatedly swooping down on their prey.

COOL FACT:

Harriers have a slight **facial disk**, which means they also depend on their ears to hunt, just like owls. As a matter of fact, they share the same habitat with Short-Eared Owls, sometimes roosting together at night.

HAWKS

Sharp-Shinned Hawk
Accipiter striatus

Sharp-Shinned Hawks are the smallest accipiter found in the United States. These raptors have short, round wings and long tails. They are very good at flying through thick forests, using their tails like rudders to make sharp, fast turns. Adults have deep red eyes, and immature birds have yellow ones. These feisty little hawks have very thin, almost stick-like legs, and weigh between three and eight ounces.

COOL FACT:

Sharp-Shinned Hawks only eat small birds. So they've learned to watch for busy bird feeders in cities and suburbs, zipping into backyards to grab their dinners!

Cooper's Hawk
Accipiter cooperii

The Cooper's Hawk looks almost exactly like the Sharp-Shinned Hawk, except it is larger. In the accipiters, the female can be nearly twice as large as the male, so a female "Sharpie" is almost as large as a male Cooper's Hawk, but not quite. Because Cooper's Hawks are larger, they are able to catch mammals like chipmunks and ground squirrels, as well as songbirds. One way to tell these two hawks apart is to look at their tails when perched. The tip of the Cooper's Hawk tail is curved when folded, and the Sharp-Shinned Hawk's tail is squared off.

COOL FACT:

The Cooper's Hawk is named for New York ornithologist William Cooper.

Northern Goshawk
Accipiter gentilis

The Northern Goshawk is the largest accipiter in the US. They are secretive, beautiful birds, with ghostly gray feathers and piercing, blood red eyes. Goshawks nest in mature forests of aspen and different species of pine trees. They will catch birds like jays, woodpeckers and grouse, as well as hunt tree and ground squirrels. When chasing prey through the forest, the Goshawk will recklessly crash through brush and fly relentlessly, not stopping until the prey is caught, or disappears from view.

COOL FACT:

The word "Goshawk" comes from the Anglo-Saxon words for "goose" and "hawk". Goshawks have been trained for hundreds of years to catch geese and ducks to feed their falconers.

Harris' Hawk
Parabuteo unicinctus

The Harris' Hawk is found in the desert southwest of the United States. They are fairly common in states like Arizona and Texas, and are well adapted to life in the desert. Harris' Hawks will build nests in tall saguaro cacti, somehow learning how to perch on them without getting too many spines stuck in their feet. These hawks are not true **buteos**; they have the long, broad wings for soaring, but their tails are also long, like accipiters. This means that Harris' Hawks can turn very quickly while chasing rabbits and quail through the desert.

COOL FACT:

Harris' Hawks are social birds, living in large family groups like a pack of wolves or a pride of lions. They help each other hunt, raise babies, and guard their territories.

Swallow-Tailed Kite
Elanoides forficatus page 18

Mississippi Kite
Ictinia mississippiensis page 19

White-Tailed Kite
Elanus leucurus page 20

Gyrfalcon
Falco rusticolus page 21

Peregrine Falcon
Falco peregrinus page 22

Prairie Falcon
Falco mexicanus page 23

Aplomado Falcon
Falco femoralis page 24

Merlin
Falco columbarius page 25

American Kestrel
Falco sparverius page 26

Crested Caracara
Caracara plancus page 27

Northern Harrier
*Circus cyaneu*s page 28

Sharp-Shinned Hawk
Accipiter striatus page 29

Cooper's Hawk
Accipiter cooperii page 30

Northern Goshawk
Accipiter gentilis page 31

Harris' Hawk
Parabuteo unicinctus page 32

Red-Tailed Hawk
Buteo jamaicensis page 33

Swainson's Hawk
Buteo swainsoni page 34

Ferruginous Hawk
Buteo regalis page 35

Rough-Legged Hawk
Buteo lagopus page 36

Red-Shouldered Hawk
Buteo lineatus page 37

Broad-Winged Hawk
Buteo platypterus page 38

Short-Tailed Hawk
Buteo brachyurus page 39

White-Tailed Hawk
Buteo albicaudatus page 40

Gray Hawk
Asturina nitida page 41

Zone-Tailed Hawk
Buteo albonotatus page 42

Common Black Hawk
Buteogallus anthracinus page 43

Great Horned Owl
Bubo virginianus page 44

Long-Eared Owl
Asio otus page 45

Short-Eared Owl
Asio flammeus page 46

Red-Tailed Hawk
Buteo jamaicensis

The Red-Tailed Hawk is the most widespread hawk in the United States. They are very adaptable and can live in almost any kind of habitat except the tundra and very large forests. Although mammals are their main prey, Red-Tailed Hawks will hunt birds, including ducks, reptiles and large insects. Some hawks that live in or near cities have even learned to stoop at pigeons, just like falcons do!

COOL FACT:

Not all Red-Tailed Hawks have red tails! When the birds are younger than one year old, they have brownish-gray tails with dark brown stripes.

Swainson's Hawk
Buteo swainsoni

Swainson's Hawks live in the western United States during the spring and summer months. Their wings are two-toned underneath, with a light front edge and a dark trailing, or back edge. This makes them very easy to spot while soaring over a field. Most Swainson's hawks also have a brown "bib" under their throats, and it looks like they were messy while eating a chocolate sundae! Because they have smaller feet than other buteos, they eat many insects like grasshoppers, as well as mammals, birds and reptiles.

COOL FACT:

The Swainson's Hawk is a true long distance flier. They migrate to Argentina during the winter months. For the birds which live in Canada, that's a 10,000 mile trip one way!

Ferruginous Hawk
Buteo regalis

The species name of this hawk, *regalis*, means "regal" or "royal". Ferruginous Hawks are the largest soaring hawk in the United States, and have a very regal look about them. Their common name comes from the Latin word *ferrugo* meaning "rust", which refers to the color on their legs. An easy way to identify these hawks in flight is to look for the rusty V-shape their legs make against their large, white bodies. The Ferruginous Hawk also has a very large mouth, and since raptors pant just like dogs to keep cool, the wide mouth of this raptor helps prevents it from getting too hot out on the open prairie.

COOL FACT:

Pairs of Ferruginous Hawks will cooperate and hunt prairie dogs together. One bird soars high overhead, distracting the prairie dog, while the second hawk flies very fast along the ground. At the last instant, this hawk pops over a mound, snatching the prey which has been looking up at the first hawk! Both birds then share the meal together.

Rough-Legged Hawk
Buteo lagopus

Have you ever worn big, fuzzy slippers to keep your feet warm? That's what this hawk does! They're called Rough-Legged because their legs are covered with feathers, right down to the tops of their feet. These hawks nest on the tundra way up north at the Arctic Circle. The ground is frozen all year, and trees cannot grow. But having leg feathers helps to keep these birds warm during the cold spring. During the fall and winter, Rough-Legged Hawks migrate to the western United States. Their small feet are perfect for hunting mice and voles.

COOL FACT:

The coloration between male and female Rough-Legged Hawks differs greatly. Usually you can tell males from females just by looking. But every once in a while there is a female "roughie" with male-colored feathers, and males which look like the females, only smaller!

Red-Shouldered Hawk
Buteo lineatus

The Red-Shouldered Hawk lives in the eastern half of the United States, and there is another subspecies that lives along the California and Oregon coasts. They are smaller than other buteos, and sort of behave and look like accipiters. Their tails are longer, with several black and white stripes, and they tend to hunt and live in forests and woodlands. Red-Shouldered Hawks catch many types of prey, including mammals, birds, reptiles and insects. They like to live near water, because they also feed on frogs, salamanders and crayfish. The call of the Red-Shouldered Hawk can be perfectly imitated by the Blue Jay, which sometimes confuses bird watchers!

COOL FACT:

Red-Shouldered Hawks have been seen eating suet (chunks of fat mixed with seeds) at bird feeders. Scientists think they may be looking for extra energy and fat when the weather is cold.

Broad-Winged Hawk
Buteo platypterus

The Broad-Winged Hawk is the smallest buteo in the United States. Their diet and habitat are very similar to the Red-Shouldered Hawk, but they don't eat quite as many amphibians. Broad-Winged Hawks migrate to Central and South America during the winter months. In the early 1900s, before raptors were protected by law, thousands of Broad-Winged Hawks were shot every year while migrating, especially at a high place in Pennsylvania called Hawk Mountain. This place is now a raptor sanctuary. Fortunately, these hawks did not become extinct, and it is now illegal to shoot ANY raptor in the United States.

COOL FACT:

The word platypterus means "wide wing" in Latin. What other word does that remind you of? How about platypus? Platypuses have wide bills, and these hawks have wide wings!

Short-Tailed Hawk
Buteo brachyurus

This is another small buteo found in the United States. The average weight is about 15 ounces, or less than one pound! Most of these hawks live in Central and South America, and Mexico. In the United States, they are found only in Florida, building nests in very tall trees in or near swamps and marshlands. Although they will eat small mammals, reptiles and amphibians, the Short-Tailed Hawk is also an excellent bird hunter, catching lots of meadowlarks and blackbirds.

COOL FACT:

Short-Tailed Hawks come in two colors or morphs. One is mostly dark brown, and the other is mostly white. Even though they look very different, they are still the same species.

White-Tailed Hawk
Buteo albicaudatus

In the United States, this hawk is found only on the coastal prairies of Texas. Their wings are very broad in the middle, pointed on the tips, and are very narrow where they attach to the body. White-Tailed Hawks do not migrate, like many other American buteos, probably because they can find enough prey to survive the mild winters of south Texas. They not only eat mammals, but birds, insects and reptiles as well. These resourceful hawks will also gather at the edges of grassfires to catch fleeing animals.

COOL FACT:

White-Tailed Hawks will eat almost anything they can catch. They've been seen eating everything from crabs to roadrunners, and will even steal food from White-Tailed Kites!

Gray Hawk

Asturina nitida

The word *nitida* means "shining" in Latin. If you are ever lucky enough to see one of these pretty little hawks in the wild, sitting in the Arizona sun, you might think they really do shine! They have gray heads and backs, and dark gray flecks on their chests and bellies. Gray Hawks are found near running water, where they find lots of lizards to eat, which are attracted to the moisture. These hawks also eat snakes, and occasionally small birds, but reptiles are definitely their favorite!

COOL FACT:

The Gray Hawk lays very few eggs compared to other hawks in the United States. The average **clutch** size is just two eggs, and sometimes they only lay one.

Zone-Tailed Hawk
Buteo albonotatus

Zone-Tailed Hawks are slender, large buteos that are almost completely black. They have four white bands on their tails, with the bottom one being the widest. Found in Arizona, New Mexico and Texas, these hawks like open country with steep canyons and sparse woodlands. Zone-Tailed Hawks hunt mammals, birds, and reptiles, and there are reports of them attacking people who've gotten too close to their nests.

COOL FACT:

The Zone-Tailed Hawk will **mimic** the rocking, unsteady flight of the Turkey Vulture, and fly with them while hunting. They even look a little like vultures, with narrow, two-toned wings. Since many prey animals, like Harris' antelope squirrels, know that Turkey Vultures won't attack them, they often ignore Zone-Tailed Hawks until it's too late!

Common Black Hawk
Buteogallus anthracinus

Despite its name, the Common Black Hawk is not very common. In the United States, they're found only in southern Arizona, New Mexico, and a very tiny portion of Texas. These jet-black hawks love to live in wet habitats, because most of their prey is aquatic, such as amphibians, crustaceans, and even fish! Common Black Hawks will also feed on reptiles, but catch very few mammals or birds. They have long legs with tough scales on them, which probably help deflect snake bites.

COOL FACT:
The Common Black Hawk will sometimes wade into the water to catch fish. They'll stand very still, until the fish get close enough, then reach out quickly with a foot and grab their meal.

OWLS

Great Horned Owl
Bubo virginianus

This is the most common owl found in the United States. They can live in almost any kind of habitat, from the frozen tundra of Alaska, down to the steamy jungles of the Amazon rain forest in South America. Great Horned Owls are very adaptable, and will eat nearly anything from mammals, including bats, to insects, fish, amphibians, even other raptors! They will also catch skunks, porcupines and rattlesnakes. They are very powerful birds, weighing up to four pounds with a four and a half-foot wingspan. These owls often take over an old raven or magpie nest, and will breed and hunt in cities and suburbs. Most of the time, you see them at dawn and dusk, which makes them more **crepuscular** than **nocturnal**.

COOL FACT:

The Great Horned Owl doesn't have real horns on its head. The long feather tufts, which some people think look like horns or ears, are simply feathers which go up or down, depending on the owl's mood.

Long-Eared Owl

Asio otus

Long-Eared Owls look a bit like Great-Horned Owls, but they are much smaller, with rusty facial disks and "ears" spaced closer together. They sleep in woodlands during the day, sometimes in small groups, and hunt over open fields and marshes at night. Their main food is small mammals like voles, mice and shrews, but they will also catch insects.

COOL FACT:

This is one of the few American owls that will actually build a nest. They use sticks, bark, and even bits of trash, and line the inside with feathers.

Short-Eared Owl
Asio flammeus

With a name like Short-Eared Owl, you can guess that the feather tufts on these birds are very small. As a matter of fact, they are hardly visible unless you are really close, and the ears are standing straight up. Short-Eared Owls will hunt during the day, especially in the late afternoon. This owl will lay between 3 to 18 eggs, depending on rodent populations. If prey is abundant, they will have lots of babies. But if prey is scarce, food for the young will be hard to find, so the owls lay fewer eggs.

COOL FACT:
The Short-Eared Owl is the only owl native to the Hawaiian Islands.

Western Screech Owl/Eastern Screech Owl
Megascops kennicottii/Megascops asio

Screech Owls are small owls with feather tufts. The Western Screech Owl is found from the Pacific coast to the Great Plains. This species is gray, with black and white markings, and yellow eyes. The Eastern Screech Owl range begins where the Western one leaves off, but scientists aren't exactly sure where the dividing line is. The Eastern Screech can be either gray, or a rusty red color. Their calls are often a series of whistles or trills, which sound like a screeching noise. There is also another similar species called the Whiskered Screech Owl (*Megascops trichopsis*). It is slightly smaller than the other Screech Owls, and is found in the very southern part of Arizona and into Mexico.

COOL FACT:

A pair of gray Eastern Screech Owls will only have gray young. But a red pair, or a mixed pair (one of each color) of owls, may have babies that are all red, all gray or some of each!

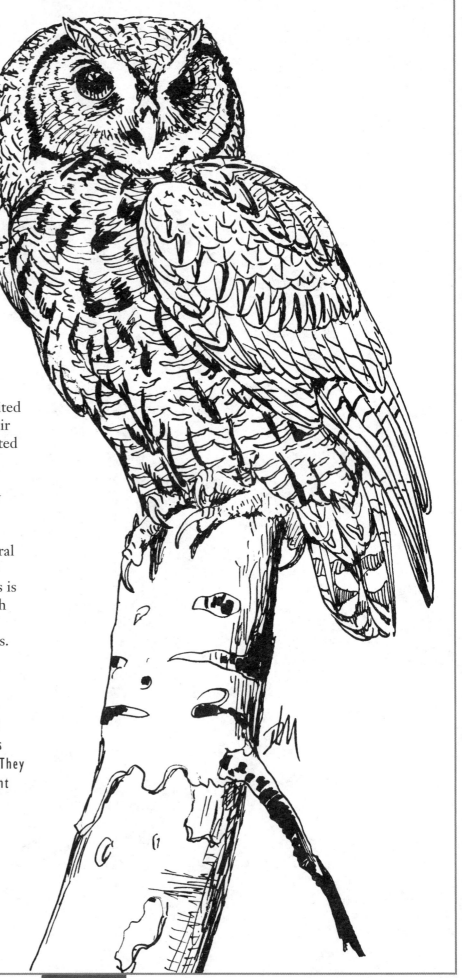

Flammulated Owl
Otus flammeolus

These are the smallest owls in the United States with feather tufts or "ears" on their heads. Like the Screech Owl, Flammulated Owls may also be rusty or red in color. They are found in mountains and woodlands from California to the Rocky Mountains, south to Mexico, but only during the spring and summer months. During the winter they migrate to Central America. One way to tell the difference between Flammulated and Screech Owls is to look at the color of their eyes: Screech Owls' eyes are yellow, and Flammulated Owls have dark brown, almost black eyes.

COOL FACT:

If Flammulated Owls sense danger, they will stand up as tall as possible, close their eyes half way and make themselves look skinny. They are trying to blend in with their environment (usually a tree) and not be seen.

Snowy Owl
Bubo scandiacus

The Snowy Owl is found all around the world above the Arctic Circle. They are among the most powerful owls in the world, with thick feathers on their legs, feet and toes. Lemmings are their favorite food, but in order to survive in the severe cold, they will catch fish, hares, birds and even scavenge around dumps. Like Short-Eared Owls, the size of a Snowy Owl clutch will depend on rodent populations, and range between 3 to 13 young. When rodent numbers are low, the owls migrate into the United States, and have been seen as far south as Texas and Georgia.

COOL FACT:

For thousands of years, Eskimos and other native Arctic peoples have hunted Snowy Owls and their eggs for food. This makes the owls very wary of people, and they spook easily if approached.

Great Gray Owl
Strix nebulosa

This huge, gray ghost of the north is the largest owl in North America, by size. Its wingspan is about four feet, and it may stand two and a half feet tall. Because they live in forests, Great Gray Owls are shaped a bit like accipiters, with shorter wings and long tails. Even though they are capable of killing larger prey like rabbits, these owls mostly hunt mice and gophers. Most Great Gray Owls live in Canada and Alaska, but sometimes they wander very far south to find food. People in the U.S. often see them hunting during the day, something they're used to doing because of the 24-hour sunlight during the Arctic summer.

COOL FACT:

Great Gray Owls will build stick nests high in aspen or evergreen trees. They line the insides with feathers and even deer hair!

Barred Owl
Strix varia

The Barred Owl also has a body shape designed for flying through forests, and is the owl featured on the cover of this book. Besides eating mammals, they are fond of aquatic prey, such as fish, amphibians and crayfish. Most Barred Owls live in the eastern U.S. but they are expanding their range north and west, where they now compete with the Northern Spotted Owl (*Strix occidentalis*) in parts of Oregon and Washington. The Barred Owl is slightly larger and more aggressive than its western cousin, and will sometimes even kill young Northern Spotted Owls in the nest.

COOL FACT:

The territorial hooting call of the Barred Owl sounds like "who cooks for you, who cooks for you all". They also make a noise that sounds like a barking dog.

Spotted Owl
Strix occidentalis

The Spotted Owl is an endangered species, mostly due to loss of habitat in the Pacific Northwest. These owls need to live in dense, mature pine forests, and these "old growth" forests are often cut down for the timber industry. For many years, scientists and government officials have been trying to find ways for both the Spotted Owl and people who need jobs to live together. But now an even greater threat may be from the Barred Owl (*Strix varia*), which has expanded its range into the Spotted Owl's habitat. Barred Owls seem to be much more adaptable. They can live in places and eat animals that the Spotted Owl can't, and they often drive Spotted Owls away from good nesting sites.

COOL FACT:

Spotted Owls are timid and sensitive to noise. Human noise, even far from their nests, can cause them to abandon their eggs and young.

Barn Owl
Tyto alba

The Barn Owl is found all over the world, on every continent except Antarctica. They have a distinct, heart-shaped face, formed by a stiff facial disk. Barn Owls have some of the best hearing of any animal, and are able to hear an insect crawling on a blade of grass 100 yards away. Their facial disks help them hear by trapping and funneling sounds to their ears. The ear openings have slightly different shapes to help them gather sound waves, and one ear is located slightly higher than the other. This allows the sound to arrive a split second apart, which enables the owl to better locate where the sound is coming from. Barn Owls like to lay eggs in cavities, and often use old barns and abandoned buildings for raising their young. They are excellent hunters of small mammals such as mice, voles and gophers.

COOL FACT:

Some legends of haunted houses may have come from Barn Owls. They don't hoot, but make a wide range of noises, including a high-pitched scream. People may have thought they'd seen a ghost as a screaming, white Barn Owl suddenly flew by them in the dark!

Northern Pygmy Owl
Glaucidium gnoma

Pygmy Owls live in western North America, but in the United States, the Ferruginous Pygmy Owl is only found in deserts in extreme southern Arizona and Texas. Although these two species look very similar, one way to tell them apart is by looking at their heads. The Northern Pygmy Owl has whitish spots on its head, but the Ferruginous Pygmy Owl has streaks. Both owls have very large feet for their size, and often kill birds nearly as big as themselves, as well as mammals and small reptiles.

Ferruginous Pygmy Owl
Glaucidium brasilianum

COOL FACT:

Both the Ferruginous and Northern Pygmy Owls have "eye spots" on the back of their necks. These are two patches of black feathers, ringed with white ones, which look like large eyes. This is protective coloration designed to fool a potential predator into thinking that the owls are looking right at them!

Elf Owl

Micrathene whitneyi

The Elf Owl lives in deserts and canyons of Arizona, New Mexico, Texas and Mexico. They have very short tails that are barely visible beneath their wings. Elf Owls sometimes lay their eggs in holes made by Gila Woodpeckers in saguaro cactus, and the spiny plant provides good protection from predators. When hunting at night, they will fly low, skimming the grass to catch insects, their main prey. Elf Owls will also eat scorpions and small tarantulas.

COOL FACT:

The Elf Owl is the smallest raptor in the United States. It measures about 5¾ inches long, and males may weigh as little as 1¼ ounces!

Northern Saw-Whet Owl
Aegolius acadicus

The Northern Saw-Whet Owl is one of the few owls in the United States that has an immature plumage. Owls less than one year old are a solid rusty-brown on the breasts and bellies. They live in very dense forests, sleeping next to tree trunks during the day and hunting at night. Their feet are also large in proportion to their body size, which means they can kill prey like songbirds and bats. Bird watchers and others have reported that Northern Saw-Whet Owls seem unafraid of people and can be approached closely in the wild.

COOL FACT:

Northern Saw-Whet Owls get their name from one of their calls. The raspy noise sounds like a saw being sharpened on a whet stone.

Boreal Owl
Aegolius funereus

The Boreal Owl looks very similar to the Northern Saw-Whet Owl, but has darker wings and a pale beak. Most live in the dense northern forests of Canada, but a few will migrate south to the United States. Small populations of these birds have recently been discovered high in the Rocky Mountains of Colorado and Wyoming, very far south of their normal range. Boreal Owls make a wailing call, which sounds like crying at a funeral, and that's where their species name comes from!

COOL FACT:

Boreal Owls sometimes seek shelter in buildings such as barns and even igloos during very severe winter storms.

Northern Hawk Owl
Surnia ulula

Northern Hawk Owls are very unusual looking birds whose bodies look more falcon than owl-like. Their tails are long, and their facial disks aren't as well-developed as other owls'. Unlike other smaller owls which tend to hide in trees during the day, Northern Hawk Owls will perch boldly at the tops of spruce trees, looking for prey. They will eat animals the size of young snowshoe hares and ruffed grouse, and are also able to hover, like American Kestrels, while searching for food.

COOL FACT:

The Northern Hawk Owl has learned to hunt in fields where bales of hay are being loaded into trucks. When a bale is lifted out of the grass, mice hiding underneath it scatter, and the waiting Hawk Owl grabs an easy meal.

Burrowing Owl
Athene cunicularia

These unusual little owls have long legs and spend much of their time on the ground. Because they are **diurnal** and rely more on their eyes for hunting, their facial disks are very faint. Burrowing Owls don't actually dig their own burrows, but will use their feet and even wings to enlarge an existing hole. They lay their eggs in these holes and tunnels dug by other creatures such as prairie dogs. Burrowing Owls live in small colonies, so sometimes several owls will be seen standing on the prairie together, often very close to prairie dog towns. When danger approaches, they make an alarm call which sounds like the rattle of a rattlesnake.

COOL FACT:

Occasionally, Burrowing Owls use dried cattle or horse droppings to line their burrows, beginning at the entrance and running all the way to the nest. Scientists think this may disguise their scent, and fool potential predators such as coyotes and badgers.

RAPTORS & HUMANS: FALCONRY

One day, around five thousand years ago, a hunter somewhere in Asia was searching for game. Perhaps he was living in what is today Mongolia, or he might have been further west, in present-day Kyrgyzstan. Scanning the vast grasslands for animals, he spotted a raptor. He had seen them before, flying effortlessly in the cold sky, and sitting in high, inaccessible places. But this time, he witnessed something extraordinary: the raptor suddenly dove, and killed an animal close to where the man was hiding. Envious of its success, and always on the brink of starvation, the man ran towards the great predator, chasing it off its kill. He stuffed the fresh, warm meat into his bag, astonished at his good fortune, and ran for home.

Later, he wondered to himself if there were any way he could track these great hunters of the sky, and be able to take their kills from them more often. He discussed with the other men of his village or camp how this might be accomplished. Someone pointed out that just as they had tamed the wild horse, and had dogs which helped them scent game, perhaps these birds could be captured, raised and trained to kill game for people.

The lone hunter might have seen a peregrine or saker falcon knock a duck out of the sky that day. Or he might have even seen a great golden eagle kill a fox or hare. We will never know, but what we do know is that humans figured out how to keep eagles, hawks and falcons as trained, skilled hunting companions in order to feed themselves. The gun was still thousands of years away from being invented, and many human societies constantly faced the threat of hunger. Falconry, the sport and art of using trained raptors to hunt wild game, spread from Central Asia eastward to China and Japan, and also west and south through Russia, Europe and into the Persian Gulf countries.

Before guns, it was a useful way of putting meat on the table for poorer people, and a glorious country pastime for the wealthy. Many famous rulers throughout the ages either practiced falconry, or helped spread information about its practice across nations, empires and continents. Alexander the Great brought knowledge of Asian and Middle Eastern falconry back to ancient Macedonia. Frederick the Second of the Hohenstaufen dynasty was so completely obsessed with falconry in the 12th and 13th centuries that he brought falcons on military campaigns, and wrote a massive treatise on the subject, which is still read today. Marco Polo, the great Italian explorer, brought back incredible stories of the huge hunting parties of Kublai Khan, consisting of thousands of men, elephants, horses, dogs, falcons and even cheetahs! During the Renaissance, falconry flourished in Europe; Henry VIII, Queen Elizabeth I and Mary, Queen of Scots were all accomplished falconers and hunters.

With the invention of firearms, falconry began to become scarce as people found better and more efficient ways of obtaining wild meat. But a few people throughout Europe, and eventually America, continued to practice the ancient ways, and pass on the secrets and skills to the next generation. Today, falconry is legal in every US state except Hawaii, and there are perhaps 4000 licensed falconers in our country. The knowledge gained over thousands of years has led to the breeding of raptors in captivity, which saved the peregrine falcon from extinction. Although today's falconers use radio and even satellite telemetry, GPS and Gore-Tex™, the same basic principles of food, training and the ultimate leap of faith required to turn a raptor loose in the sky remain the same.

To find out more about falconry, visit www.N-A-F-A.org

FIDGET'S FREEDOM
Words by Stacey Patterson • Illustrations by Vadim Gorbartov

10" x 10" casebound, 32 pages, ISBN 0-9723422-6-5, $17.95

Fidget is a young peregrine falcon eager to try out her newly feathered wings. She and her brother Echo had been hatched in an incubator in a laboratory and are now living in a "hack" box nestled on a cliff. This will be their home until they can hunt and fend for themselves. Their caretakers, both falconers and scientists, had become concerned about the plight of the peregrine due to the use of DDT in North America. DDT caused egg shell thinning and without intervention, extinction in some of their native territories was a possibility. When the box is opened to release the birds, Fidget, the bolder of the two throws caution to the wind as she takes to her wings — and soon finds more than she bargained for on her first flight. *Fidget's Freedom* is published in cooperation with the Raptor Education Foundation whose mission is to advance environmental literacy through educational programs, books, research services, and their website: www.usaref.org.

Available from your local bookseller, or complete the order form below to order directly from the publisher.

Please send me _____ copies of *Fidget's Freedom* @ $17.95 each $_____

Domestic orders please add $4.00 per book for shipping and handling $_____

ORDER TOTAL $_____

We accept ❏ VISA, ❏ MasterCard, and ❏ American Express Credit Card Number: _____

Expiration Date: _____ Cardholder's Signature _____

Name _____

Address _____

City _____ State _____ Zip/Postal Code _____

Country _____ **Telephone Number _____

Please send a completed form to Moonlight Publishing LLC, 2528 Lexington Street, Lafayette, CO 80026, fax to (303)664-1439, or email the required information to moonlightpubllc@msn.com.

*Within the continental United States.

International orders will require an additional $4.00 shipping and handling charge.

**We are sorry, but we absolutely cannot process a credit card order without a valid telephone number.

We respect your privacy and will not disclose this information to any third parties.

BUILD A KESTREL BOX . . . *It's Easy*

MATERIALS LIST:

Weatherproof plywood, or heavy fiberboard—make sure that the material is not treated with arsenic based chemicals which are often used for insect/water protection—¼" thickness is adequate.

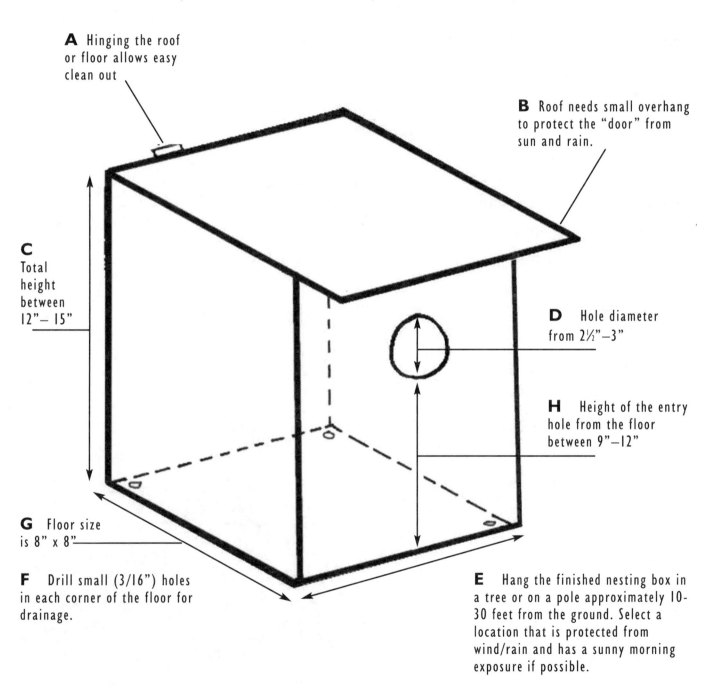

A Hinging the roof or floor allows easy clean out

B Roof needs small overhang to protect the "door" from sun and rain.

C Total height between 12"–15"

D Hole diameter from 2½"–3"

H Height of the entry hole from the floor between 9"–12"

G Floor size is 8" x 8"

F Drill small (3/16") holes in each corner of the floor for drainage.

E Hang the finished nesting box in a tree or on a pole approximately 10-30 feet from the ground. Select a location that is protected from wind/rain and has a sunny morning exposure if possible.

Make sure all your edges and surfaces are smooth so that your Kestrel will not snag feathers or toes. Just remember, you may not always get a Kestrel. Other birds may also occupy your box. Place it securely and safely (other predators may want to get at the babies) and begin your observations to see who will enjoy your gift.

BIBLIOGRAPHY

Terres, John K. *The Audubon Society Encyclopedia of North American Birds*, Alfred A. Knopf, New York, New York, 1956. 1109 pages

Grossman, Marie Louise and Hamlet, John. *Birds of Prey of the World*. Bonanza Books, New York, New York, 1964, 496 pages

Amadon, Dean and Brown, Leslie. *Eagles, Hawks, and Falcons of the World*. Wellfleet Press, Secaucus, New Jersey, 1989. 945 pages

Weidensaul, Scott. *The Raptor Almanac*. The Lyons Press, New York, New York, 2000, 382 pages.

Johnsgard, Paul A. *Hawks, Eagles and Falcons of North America*. Smithsonian Institution Press, Washington D.C., 1990, 403 pages

Baptista, Luis and Welty, Joel Carl. *The Life of Birds*. Saunders College Publishing, New York, New York, 1988, 581 pages

Wheeler, Brian K. and Clark, William S. *A Photographic Guide to North American Raptors*. Academic Press Limited, San Diego, California, 1996, 198 pages

Wheeler, Brian K. and Clark, William S. *Peterson Field Guides: Hawks*. Houghton Mifflin Company, Boston, Massachussetts, 1987, 195 pages

ABOUT THE AUTHOR

Anne Price's passion in life is raptors; she began working with them when she was 12 years old.

She grew up in the San Francisco Bay Area, volunteering at Marine World Africa USA, and received her falconry license when she was 16. She graduated from the University of Colorado with a B. A. in Environmental, Population and Organismic Biology. As an environmental scientist with Bechtel Corporation, she worked on a variety of projects, including Denver International Airport. She has been with the Raptor Education Foundation since 1986, where she serves as Curator and heads the docent program. She shares her home in Littleton, Colorado with her husband, two children, a Standard Schnauzer, a Harris' Hawk and Merlin.

Anne is pictured above with her favorite REF bird. Their relationship goes back to 1980. That's when Anne first "met" this male golden eagle, when she was only 12 years old. Four years later, at 16, she started handling him. This eagle was originally captured from the wild around 1955 as a young adult bird, which makes him the oldest raptor REF cares for.